A Spider
in My Bedroom

Story by Leone Peguero

Illustrations by Sharyn Madder

One morning, when Alex woke up,
she saw something on the wall
at the end of her bed.
She stared at it.

"Oh, no!" she whispered.
"It's a great big spider!"

Alex told herself
she was going to be brave.
After all,
it wasn't very close to her.
But was it far enough away?

"Stay right where you are!"
she said to the spider.

Alex leaped out of bed
and hurried into the kitchen.

"Mom!" she cried.
"There's an enormous spider
in my bedroom."

"Most spiders won't hurt you, Alex,"
said Mom.
"Take a plastic jar and catch it."

"Oh, I couldn't do that!" said Alex.

Mom said, "All you have to do
is put a jar over it,
and slide some paper underneath.
Then the spider will be caught
in the jar,
and you can let it go.
Spiders are happier outside."

Mom and Alex
went into the bedroom,
but the spider had gone.

"It was right there," said Alex,
pointing to the spot.

They looked everywhere for it.

"Where could it be?" Alex wondered.
It was scary
not being able to find a spider
when you knew it was really there.

"It's time to get ready
for school, Alex," said Mom.
"Don't worry. I'll find it
before you get home."

But as Alex got dressed
she kept looking around,
just in case the spider came back.

At school,
Alex couldn't stop thinking
about the spider.
She looked so upset
that the teacher asked her
what the matter was.

"There's an enormous spider
in my bedroom," said Alex.
"I'm scared of it."

"Oh, I do understand," said the teacher.
"But spiders hunt insects,
and that's a very good thing."

"I know," said Alex.
"But I wish it would hunt for insects
outside my bedroom."

"Did you catch the spider?"
Alex asked Mom when she got home.

"Sorry," said Mom. "I couldn't find it.
But don't worry about it.
It might not come back."

That night,
Alex didn't want to sleep
in her bedroom.
To make her feel better,
Mom found an insect net,
and put it carefully around the bed.

Early the next morning,
Alex lifted the net and peeped out.
The spider had come back!
There it was,
in the same place on the wall.

"Oh, no!" whispered Alex.

It was too early to wake Mom.
And anyway, the spider might disappear
before she got there.

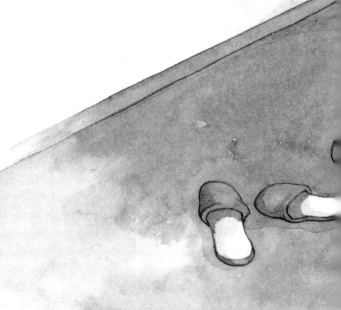

Alex knew she had to catch the spider.
And she would have to do it
by herself.

First, she opened the window.
Then she picked up the jar
and walked slowly toward the wall.

She placed it over the spider,
and slid the paper carefully underneath.

She had caught the spider at last!

Alex ran to the window
and shook the jar.

"Happy hunting!"
she called to the spider,
as it hurried off into the bushes...
outside her bedroom.

FUR

by Eric Geron

Children's Press®
An imprint of Scholastic Inc.

Library of Congress Cataloging-in-Publication Data

Names: Geron, Eric, author.
Title: Fur / by Eric Geron.
Description: First edition. | New York : Children's Press, an imprint of
  Scholastic Inc., 2024. | Series: Learn about: animal coverings |
  Includes index. | Audience: Ages 5–7. | Audience: Grades K–1. | Summary:
  "Let's learn all about the different types of animal coverings! Animals
  have different body coverings for different reasons. Some animals use
  their coverings to keep warm or stay cool, others use them for
  protection, and can either stand out or blend in. Some animals even use
  their coverings to move! This vibrant new set of LEARN ABOUT books gives
  readers a close-up look at five different animal coverings, from fur and
  feathers to skin, scales, and shells. Each book is packed with
  photographs and fun facts that explore how each covering suits the
  habitat, diet, survival, and life cycle of various animals in the
  natural world. Which animals have fur? Mammals! Do you know why mammals
  need fur to survive? With amazing photos and lively text, this book
  explains how fur helps mammals stay dry, keep warm, defend themselves,
  and more! Get ready to learn all about fur!"—Provided by publisher.
Identifiers: LCCN 2023000185 (print) | LCCN 2023000186 (ebook) |
  ISBN 9781338898026 (library binding) | ISBN 9781338898033 (paperback) |
  ISBN 9781338898040 (ebook)
Subjects: LCSH: Fur—Juvenile literature. | Body covering
  (Anatomy)—Juvenile literature. | Animals—Adaptations—Juvenile
  literature. | BISAC: JUVENILE NONFICTION / Animals / General | JUVENILE
  NONFICTION / Science & Nature / General (see also headings under Animals
  or Technology)
Classification: LCC QL942 .G47 2024 (print) | LCC QL942 (ebook) | DDC
  591.47—dc23/eng/20230110
LC record available at https://lccn.loc.gov/2023000185
LC ebook record available at https://lccn.loc.gov/2023000186

10 9 8 7 6 5 4 3 2 1   24 25 26 27 28
Printed in China   62

First edition, 2024
Book design by Kay Petronio

Photos ©: cover: AlexTurton/Getty Images; 8 background:
Byrdyak/Getty Images; 8 bottom inset: Stuart Westmorland/
Getty Images; 11 top: Momatiuk Eastcott/Animals Animals/
age fotostock; 12–13: Alastair Pollock Photography/Getty
Images; 15: Cheryl Ramalho/Getty Images; 17: JNevitt/
Getty Images; 24 center left: Chris Blank/Getty Images; 24
bottom right: fmajor/Getty Images; 25: Gunther Fraulob/
Alamy Images; 29 top left: Wesley Vroom/500px/Getty
Images; 29 top right: Wolfgang Kaehler/Getty Images; 29
center right: Jupiterimages/Getty Images.

All other photos © Shutterstock.

A special thank-you
to the team at the
Cincinnati Zoo &
Botanical Garden
for their expert
consultation.

CONTENTS

INTRODUCTION

Thick as Fur

Animal bodies can have different coverings. Some are covered with feathers. Others are covered with skin, scales, or shells. This book is all about a special covering: fur! Fur can be short or long, curly or straight, spotted or striped.

LEOPARD

Fur grows in many colors and patterns.
Discover which animals have it, what fur is
made of, and the fantastic things it can do.

Which Animals Have Fur?

Mammals have fur! Mammals are **warm-blooded** animals. Did you know humans are mammals? All mammals have **backbones** and breathe air.

Fur and hair are made from keratin, the same material that makes up human nails and bird feathers.

Mammals live on every continent. Some live on land, and some live in water.

Did you know fur and hair are the same thing? We usually say that hair is what grows on humans. Fur is what grows on mammals that are not humans.

CHAPTER 1

Special Fur

Fur is really useful. Just like there are different types of mammals, there are also different types of fur. Each type of fur plays an important role. Some fur protects against sunburn and scrapes.

Certain types of mammals are hairless—like dolphins and whales!

BOTTLENOSE DOLPHIN

Close-up of brown bear fur

BROWN BEAR

Some fur keeps mammals dry in the water. Sometimes fur helps a mammal stay warm or cool off. Some fur hides a mammal from **predators** or **prey**. Some fur can even sense danger!

FUR SEAL

Fur

This is a fur seal. It uses its fur to stay warm
in cold weather. Like most mammals, its fur
has a topcoat and an undercoat. Topcoats
are made of long, oily hairs that protect
against harsh wind, icy water, and hot sun.

Topcoat

Undercoat

The topcoat is made of guard hairs, and the undercoat is made of down hairs.

Panda bear fur also has a topcoat and undercoat.

Undercoats are made of soft, short, thick hairs that help keep animals from getting chilly or overheated.

CHAPTER 2

Fur to the Rescue

Sometimes mammals are outside in the rain. The topcoat acts like a rain jacket by protecting the undercoat from getting wet. If the undercoat gets wet, the mammal will become too cold.

BEAVER

Water slides off the topcoat of a beaver because the hairs are coated in oil.

FUR SEAL

Fur also lets certain mammals swim and be underwater without getting soaked. The topcoat also acts like a windbreaker by protecting mammals from wind.

Sunproof

Fur does a great job at protecting mammals from getting a sunburn. The fur blocks sunlight from burning their skin. Mammals with only a small amount of fur have a higher chance of getting a sunburn.

Hippos create a pinkish oil that coats their skin as an added layer of protection from the sun.

ASIAN ELEPHANT

Some mammals coat themselves in mud, which acts like a natural sunscreen. These animals include pigs, elephants, hippopotamuses, and rhinoceroses.

15

CHAPTER 3

Fur-mometer

Mammals use their fur to help control their body temperature. One way a mammal can keep warm is by using their fur to trap heat close to their body.

The musk ox has such thick fur that it can survive in −40°F (−40°C) temperatures!

ARCTIC FOX

The undercoat traps this warm air. The heat allows them to stay warm in the cold. By having darker-colored fur, a mammal can absorb more sunlight. This keeps them warmer than a mammal with lighter-colored fur.

Cooling Down

Believe it or not, a lot of mammals have fur that helps them to stay cool. The fur prevents them from getting too hot. Fur keeps the heat of the sun from reaching their skin.

If a camel's fur is 158°F (70°C), its skin underneath can be 104°F (40°C).

GIRAFFES

Fur that is
lighter in color
keeps cooler
than darker fur.

CHAPTER 4

Invisible Mammals

Many mammals have fur that allows them to hide in their **habitat**. The ability to blend into their surroundings is called **camouflage**. Camouflage helps protect mammals from being seen by predators or prey. A cheetah can vanish into its surroundings. Its spotted fur looks like trees and grass.

All the fur on an animal is known as its **pelage**.

CHEETAH

THREE-TOED
SLOTH

The three-toed sloth disappears into its habitat. The green **algae** growing on its fur looks like part of the trees.

Hidden Furballs

Just like certain mammals can blend in with trees and grasses, their fur color can also blend in with the snow. Having white fur allows certain animals to camouflage.

Animals like the snowshoe hare lose their brown fur for the winter. They grow white fur to help them blend in with the snow. In the spring, brown fur lets them blend into dirt and rocks after the snow has melted away.

SHORT-TAILED
WEASEL

Arctic foxes,
harp seal pups,
snowshoe hares,
and short-tailed
weasels can all
have white fur.

CHAPTER 5

What Else Can Fur Do?

Fur also helps some mammals sense what is going on around them. A mammal's whiskers are a special type of hair. They are different from the fur on its body.

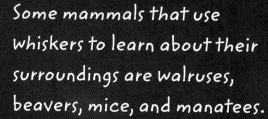

Some mammals that use whiskers to learn about their surroundings are walruses, beavers, mice, and manatees.

LION

Whiskers are thicker and stiffer than most types of hair. Whiskers help animals find food. Whiskers help animals sense danger. They can also help animals move through their surroundings. Whiskers are especially helpful for mammals who move around at night or swim through dark water.

Defenses and Warnings

Some mammals have fur that is used to defend themselves! Fur can be used as a warning sign. Did you know that porcupine **quills** are made of hair? The porcupine raises these hairs to warn threats to go away. The skunk has a white stripe down its back that warns predators of its stinky spray.

Sometimes when mammals feel upset, the hair on their bodies automatically stands up.

PORCUPINE

The honey
badger has a
stripe to warn
predators of its
fighting power.
The white-tailed
deer shakes
its tail to alert
other deer to
nearby danger.

HONEY BADGER

New Fur

All mammals **shed**, or lose fur and replace it with a new layer. Many mammals shed all their fur from the undercoat, usually when the weather warms up. A thinner coat means the mammal can keep cool during hotter days.

An average human loses 50–100 hairs a day!

German shepherds shed year-round.

These animals shed all at once.

Highland Cow

Moose

Mountain Goat

Some mammals shed a few hairs at a time year-round. Other mammals shed their layer of fur all at once. Shedding gets rid of any old fur to allow newer fur to grow.

RACCOON

Fur Matters

Now you know all about fur! It can be short and soft or long and stiff. Fur comes in different colors and patterns. Mammals need it to survive. Fur helps mammals with warmth, dryness, and protection from the sun. It also helps mammals hide from view or protect themselves from harm. Next time you see a furry animal, remember how its fur makes so many things possible for it.

The animal with the thickest fur is the sea otter, with about 1 million hairs per square inch!

GLOSSARY

algae (AL-jee) small plants without roots or stems that grow mainly in water

backbone (BAK-bohn) a set of connected bones that runs down the middle of the back; also called the spine

camouflage (KAM-uh-flahzh) a disguise or natural coloring that allows animals to hide by making them look like their surroundings

habitat (HAB-i-tat) the place where an animal or plant is usually found

keratin (KEHR-uh-tin) a fiber-like protein that forms the structure of feathers, hair, and nails

mammal (MAM-uhl) a warm-blooded animal that has hair or fur and usually gives birth to live babies

pelage (PE-lij) a mammal's fur, considered all together

predator (PRED-uh-tur) an animal that lives by hunting other animals for food

prey (pray) an animal that is hunted by another animal for food

quill (kwil) one of the hollow, sharp spines on a porcupine

shed to get rid of old feathers or fur

warm-blooded (WORM bluhd-id) having a body temperature that does not change, even if the temperature of the surroundings is very hot or very cold

INDEX

ABOUT THE AUTHOR

Eric Geron is the author of many books. He lives in New York City with his little fluffy dog, whom he refers to as his " fur baby. "